Book 1
Oil Painting
By Scott Landowski

&

Book 2
Pastel Drawing
By Scott Landowski

Book 1
Oil Painting

By Scott Landowski

1-2-3 Easy Techniques To Oil Painting

Oil Painting: 1-2-3 Easy Techniques To Mastering Oil Painting

Table of Contents

Introduction

I want to thank you and congratulate you for downloading the book, Oil Painting: 1-2-3 Easy Techniques to Mastering Oil Painting!

This book contains proven steps and strategies on how to overcome different challenges in oil painting. The step-by-step approach of this book will guide you in achieving a successful start in your oil painting practice.

This book covers the fundamentals of oil painting, the principles of mixing oil paint colors and developing an image. The simplified steps are a guarantee that even beginners will be able to relate with the process.

Thank you and we hope you enjoy this book.

Chapter 1. Oil Painting Overview

Oil painting has been around for centuries. It makes use of a kind of paint that has creamy and smooth consistency, and can produce vivid colors. When one speaks of oil painting, the image of great artists and their masterpieces also come to mind. This is a very old painting practice and though there have been a lot of changes in the materials being used, the techniques have not changed that much.

An oil paint consists of dry colored powder mixed with a drying oil as the binder; hence, the name. Some people create their own oil paints but you can buy ready to use oil paints from stores. Ready to use oil paints normally come in tubes. The oil paints are combined to make various colors.

Oil paints take time to dry. This attribute has its benefits and drawbacks. One of the benefits of using a slow drying paint is that you can refine and adjust the image that you are painting before it dries. Oil paints also make it possible for you to correct some parts of your painting that you want to remove. You can remove an image by using a wet rag, a palette knife or a rubber squeegee.

The disadvantage of using oil paints is that it can be difficult to apply different colors next to each because they can mix if you are not careful in applying them. Once a painting is finished and is completely dry a varnish is applied to protect the painting.

Mastering the art of chemistry is essential to achieving the proper effects for your work. This complexity of oil painting makes it fun and challenging to work with.

Basic Information About Painting Using Oil Paints

Most of the commercial tube paints are ready to use. In some instances, you may use a solvent or a medium to modify the paint. The solvent dilutes the paint and the medium adds oil back to the paint to make it creamy. As you spend more time working with oil paints, you will notice that some colors take more time to dry than the other colors.

After an oil paint, has been applied, it develops a skin of dry surface through the chemical process called curing. This process protects the surface of the painting.

Take note though, that the surface might be dry but the entire painting itself will takes months before it becomes thoroughly dry.

You will also discover that two colors mixed together will not look the same if they are applied in two separate overlapping layers. This is the reason that at times, you will need to wait for the first layer to dry a bit before you apply the next layer to achieve a certain color or texture. It is important for a beginner to know these qualities of oil paints for a successful painting project.

Materials Used in Oil Painting

- **Oil Paints**
  Oil paint is a type of paint that consists of a colored powder mixed with a drying oil. The most popular drying oil is linseed oil. The drying oil makes the paint dry slowly. You can buy ready to use oil paints in various colors.
- **Viewfinder**
  A viewfinder is a sighting tool that helps you create a frame for your object, just like a viewfinder on a camera. You can make one by cutting a window out an index card. The outer layer will serve as your frame. The items you see inside its window will be the same item you will paint in your canvas.
- **Canvas**
  A canvas is commonly used fabric used for painting. The fabric is usually placed in a wooden frame.
- **Easel**
  It is a self-supporting wooden frame used to hold the canvas while it is being painted or drawn.
- **Palette**
  A palette is a thin board where oil paints are mixed. It can be made of wood, plastic, ceramic or other materials. It also comes in different sizes and shapes
- **Different sizes of paintbrush**
  A paintbrush has bristles, a handle, and a ferrule. Brushes come in different sizes, shapes and have different types of bristles.
- **Palette knife**
  The palette knife is a thin steel blade with a handle and is used for mixing colors and applying or removing paint.
- **Paint thinner, turpentine, solvent or linseed oil**
  These liquid materials are used to adjust the consistency of the oil paint.

Chapter 2. Fundamentals of Oil Painting

Before you start painting, familiarize yourself first with the basics of the painting process. This means that you should study the basic shapes and colors of an image before getting into the details.

Basic Painting Process

One of the main qualities of oil painting is applying paint in layers. The first step in oil painting is to sketch in the different parts of the painting using a wash. A wash is a pale color that is made by mixing an oil paint with a solvent.

After making the sketch, apply paint in the major light and dark areas. Adjust the colors and shapes by starting with a thin layer of paint. Gradually apply thicker layers of paint to let the colors in the lower layer's peek through.

Below is a more detailed instruction of the steps:

1. Create a sketch.
    The initial marks on a canvas make up the drawing using a wash. A wash is a thin mixture of paint and solvent that is fast drying and easy to modify. You can easily make changes to your drawing at this stage. Do not use a solvent to erase or clean marks because it will just create a mess. The best way to correct part of the sketch is to wait until it slightly dries and paint over it.

2. Choose your plot.
    After you outlined the image on the canvas, you will be able to foresee the outcome of your painting. At this stage, you should still be able to make changes and improve the overall design of your painting.

3. Apply the major colors.
    Once you have finalized your design, you can block in the major colors. You can adjust on the object of your painting as you apply the major colors. Your painting takes on a more substantial appearance as you apply more colors.

4. Paint in layers.

With the basic colors in place, you can start applying heavier paint to your objects. The succeeding layers can be of the same shade of color or you may adjust it to depending on the effect that you would like to bring out in the painting.

Brushes and Brushstrokes

Brushes come in different sizes and shapes. They are usually long enough to allow you to vary the brushstrokes just by changing the way you hold the brush. For instance, if you hold the brush down by the ferrule, you use the small muscles of your hand and fingers and have fine control over the strokes. On the contrary, if you hold the brush farther away from the ferrule, you have a looser hold on the brush for loose, expressive strokes. The ferule is the metal part of the paintbrush that olds the bristles and the handle together.

Different Brush Sizes and Bristles

- Short and square-ended paintbrush makes square corners and tight edges. This brush is great for geometric shapes or manmade objects.
- Long and floppy filberts make elegant, organic, lozenge-shaped marks. This brush is perfect for organic and natural objects.
- Sable or synthetic fibers are more delicate than the bristle brushes and leave less of a mark.

Different types of Paintbrush

1. **Filbert**
   Filberts are used this to paint leaves, clouds and other living things and natural organic forms.
2. **Flat**
   This paints large areas of color. This type of paintbrush is also best for painting geometric forms and filling out square corners because it gives a clean crisp edge.
3. **Bright**
   This brush is like flat the only difference is that it is shorter, broader and holds less paint.
4. **Round**

This is great for drawing lines.

5. **Fan brushes**

   The fan brushes are used for fine blending.

6. **Extra-long filberts**

   You can use these to make very loose and expressive marks.

7. **Stencil brushes**

   You can use a stencil brush for dry brush. They are chubby and round.

8. **House painting brushes**

   Use them for big projects and for dry brushing.

9. **Foam brushes**

   You can use them pick up excess paint.

10. **Painting knife**

    This like a palette knife but it is more rigid. You can use it as a trowel to pick up paint and apply it to the canvas.

Different Glazing Techniques

A glaze is a transparent coat applied to create an illusion of a third color. It is a thin layer applied over another color. Glazing refers to any type of painting that allows you to see two different colors at the same time. You can see this definition in layers of color thinned with medium. You can also see it when paint is marked in small spots of color.

- **Imprimatura**

  This Italian term means that you start with a colored background. The typical background of a painting is white. However, there are instances wherein you will start your painting with a colored canvas. If you have a colored canvas, paint it with a fast-drying coat to bring out the undertones. Allow the area to dry a bit before you wipe away some of the paint. Create the light areas of your image by wiping them with a rag or a dry paintbrush. Let it dry thoroughly before you proceed with your painting. This technique is like using an eraser to pull out the light areas of the drawing rather than laying in dark areas.

- **Scumbling**

  It refers to removing a thin layer of a paint by applying an oil paint on it. You scrape off the excess paint until just a tiny part of it is left. This technique works well with dense colors especially if a light color is applied over a dark color.

- **Sgraffito**
  This is like scumbling; the only difference is that with sgraffito distinct marks are left. You can use this technique if you want to show defined textures or ragged edges.

- **Dry Brush**
  This technique is done on a dry part of your painting. Lightly brush over the painting using a stiff, dried paint on a dry brush. This works best and produces more specks on a rough and textured surface rather than on a smooth surface.

- **Impasto**
  This is the process of painting using a thick paint. This helps to add texture to the painting. You can use a regular oil paint or a ready to use impasto medium.

Chapter 3. Master the Art of Mixing Colors

Mixing and matching colors can be overwhelming. Mixing colors is an essential technique that every beginner must learn. Most beginners think that the best way to make something look darker is to mix it with black and to make something lighter you mix it with white. These color combinations though will not help you achieve your desired color.

The best way to learn about colors is by creating a color chart and knowing the color wheel. That way, you will discover how to make light and darks using other colors instead of just using black and white. This technique will keep you from making the mistake that most beginners commit which is creating cloudy colors. By making a color chart or wheel, you will learn how to mix the colors and begin to get a feel for applying paint to the canvas in a uniform manner.

Color Terminologies

It is important that before you make a color wheel or chart, you are familiar with the color terminologies to avoid confusions.

- **Primary Colors**
  These are red, blue and yellow.
- **Hue**
  Hue is the name of the color, such as red, green, blue, or another color. A pure hue is the brightest version of a color.
- **Tint**
  A tint is a lighter version of a hue. You make a tint by adding white to a pure hue.
- **Shade**
  A shade is a mixture of the pure hue plus black. Another way to make a shade is to use the hue's complement rather than black in these mixtures.
- **Complement**
  It is the hue directly across the color wheel from the hue that you are working with.
- **Tone**

It is a mixture of a shade plus white, or you can think of it as the pure hue plus black and white. You can also use the complement rather than black in the mixture.

Color Illusions

Once you have mastered the color wheel and the art of mixing colors, you must also familiarize about the effects of colors with each other.

- **Value and Size**
  A color in a smaller area will seem darker and brighter. An example would be the color on the cover of a paint can, if you paint an entire room with it, you will notice that the color appears lighter compared to how it appears on the cover of the can. The smaller the area that a color covers, the darker it appears.

- **Value**
  A color surrounded by a lighter color appears to be darker, but if it is surrounded by a darker color, it appears to be lighter.

- **Hue Effect**
  A color surrounded by one of its primary hues appears to be more like its other primary pure hue.

  For instance, you want to use violet in a paint. Violet is made of the primary colors red and blue. If red surrounds a violet paint, the violet paint would look like it has more blue in it. On the contrary, if blue surrounds violet, the violet paint would appear as if it has more red in it. Though, the two violets are of the same concentration.

- **Intensity**
  Complementary colors placed next to each other make each other look brighter, but similar hues make each other look duller. On the other hand, any brighter color makes another color look darker, and any dark color makes another color look brighter.

Chapter 4. Monochromatic Painting

Start with Black and White Paint

Black and white painting is a type of monochromatic painting or also known as under-painting. Monochromatic painting just uses one color or hue but in ranging values, from light, medium to dark. In black and white painting, you use different values of gray (a combination of black and white) to create your painting.

Starting your oil painting adventure in black and white makes it less overwhelming. However, it's a good way to practice as it gives you the chance to use oil paints and see how they work. This exercise is like creating a sketch.

- **Find a Still Subject**
  Look for things that are plain and simple. Choose two to three items and group them together but do not place them tightly close to each other. Place your objects in an area that will let them cast shadows.
  Arrange your objects so that the areas around them make remarkable shapes as well.

- **Draw the Initial Sketch**
  Do not use a pencil to draw the sketch on your canvas. Use a wash or a pale paint to draw your sketch. A wash is a pale color of your paint. You can create a wash by directly mixing a pool of gray oil paint in a jar of a solvent.

  Another way is you squeeze out a pool of white and black paint on your palette. Then take a small part of your white and black paint using a palette knife to create a gray mixture. Dampen a round brush with a solvent and knock off the excess solvent. Take a small amount of the gray paint. You will still end up with a wash of gray because of the solvent on the brush.

Sketch your outline using the gray wash. If you need to make corrections, use a darker shade of gray.

- **Sighting and Measuring**
  Sighting is a way of checking to see whether your objects are drawn properly. You can use your paintbrush handle to compare the actual object to the painted object. You can do this by closing one eye and holding out your paintbrush handle at arm's length and visually lay it along the edge of the item to get the angle that you are trying to draw.

- **Block Major Shadows**
  Locate the shadows of your object. Dip a brush in solvent and take some of the gray wash used for the initial sketch. Apply paint on the dark side of the objects.

- **Develop the Image**
  The basic rule of painting is that you start with the main objects first and secondary areas like the shadow and then the background. When you develop the image, you need to mix three shades of gray and use a different paintbrush for it. Using a palette knife, create a light gray, medium gray, and dark gray. Apply the medium gray first on the middle areas. Use the light grey in areas that are closer to the light and the dark gray to the shadows. As you paint the entire canvass, you can make adjustments on your objects to achieve a more polished image. It is important not to leave any part of the canvass unpainted because it will eventually turn to yellow that would ruin the effect of your painting.

Chapter 5. Paint Local Colors Using Analogous Colors

Analogous means identical or similar. You can practice painting objects by finding its analogous color in the color wheel. It can be difficult to paint objects in colors particularly for beginners. For this painting, do not use black and white colors. You use complementary colors to make something appear darker.

To practice your painting skill, start with painting a green apple, an orange and a lemon. Objects that are medium or light in color are best for this exercise. For the background, use a blue cloth.

Frame and sketch

Use a viewfinder to frame your scene and sketch the objects using a wash. Make a wash of the color with your solvent, and use the wash to draw out the objects. Make the objects nice and big or at least life-size.

You can adjust your drawing by choosing a color slightly darker that the first. Using a different color helps you keep track of which line to use when you begin to develop the painting.

Find the local color

The local color is the natural color of an object as it appears in normal light. Look at the objects you have and ask yourself what colors they are. The green apple is more yellow-green than green; the orange is orange; and the lemon is yellow.

Paint the Orange

Now mix a small pool of color to match the local color of one of your orange. You may have to adjust the actual color by using more yellow or red to get the right color.

To match color perfectly, put some of your paint on your palette knife and place it next to the object. Make sure that you hold it up to the side of the orange that is closer to the light. If you see a color in the object that is missing on the knife, add that color. For example, if your orange fruit looks more yellow than the paint on the knife, add yellow; if it looks more reddish, add red. Experiment with the colors to get the right one. It takes practice to master color combination. Just try and try and add just a little bit at a time until you get it right.

1. Choose analogous colors.

Find the color that comes the closest to the color of the orange in your still life. In this case, it will be orange. Look also for tubes of oil paints that match the color of the other parts of your orange and put them on your palette as well. You do not have to mix anything at this point. Just place the oil paints next to each other in your palette. Squeeze out small amount of yellow, red, yellowish-brown, and crimson.

2. Begin applying the color.

Take the orange paint that you made and apply a thin wash to the orange on your canvas. Cover the middle and shaded side of the orange with this color. As you get to the part of the orange that is lighter, pick up some yellow with the same brush and add it right to the canvas. It will look yellow-orange. You can also add pure yellow to the exact point where the light hits the orange.

For the shaded side, make a color that is more red-orange. Use a fresh, clean brush to apply it to the underside of the orange on your canvas. Now your orange fruit is orange with yellow highlights and a red-orange shaded side. You can use a red that has a bit of crimson for the very bottom of the orange.

3. Do not blend the colors in applying the paint instead apply them in a block.

Paint the Lemon

The lemon is a little tricky because its local color is bright yellow. It is the lightest color on the color wheel, so it functions as the highlight. With yellow objects, you should figure out which direction to move on the color chart to find the analogous color to create a shadow of yellow that looks like it belongs on a lemon. Paint the entire lemon with yellow and then move on to the shaded side.

Your analogous color options are green and orange. When you look closely at the lemon on the shaded side, you notice that it looks greenish on the darker side. So, use yellow for the highlight and yellow-green for the shaded side. Experiment with different greens for your lemon.

Paint the Green Apple

The apple on your sketch will be round, but you know that the shape of an apple is significantly different from an orange. The stem comes out on the top through a hollow part.

Using a yellow wash for your drawing, adjust the shape of the apple. Find the little indention at the top of the apple, and use your yellow to make a mark. Change it with the next analogous color, like yellow-green. Use yellow to establish the structure of the apple by making a line right through the middle of the apple as if you are stabbing it. Draw an ellipse on the top of the apple and then make a second ellipse to mark the shoulders of the apple.

The local color of the green apple is yellow-green. The apple also has yellow highlights and a green-shaded side. Use yellow, and a tiny bit of both ultramarine blue and cerulean blue.

Find the shaded side and paint it in with a thin wash of yellow-green. Continue to fill in the lights with yellow and the shaded side with green. The green is in the top indention and off to one side of the indention. Use yellow or a lighter version of yellow-green to fill in the lightest part of the green apple.

The Background

Identify the local color of your cloth first and find its analogous color. Find all the blues, blue-greens, and blue-violets that may work for your cloth. The shadows cast by the objects onto the cloth are a darker version of the color of the cloth; they have nothing to do with the color of the object casting the shadow. Take the color of the cloth and the color for the cast shadows and apply them to the painting in a thin wash.

Paint Shiny Objects

You have learned previous how to apply colors. You already know how to use colors to create a three-dimensional form. However, you have yet to learn how to paint objects that are more complicated. These are the shiny objects like a metal and a glass. In painting a shiny object, you must learn how to capture its glimmer and glow.

Paint Metal

Start with a simple metal subject like a tin can. You can find it anywhere and it is very easy to draw in terms of shape. You can paint an image of the can by itself, or make a small still life with the can. Place the can on a surface with some color and experiment with the lighting and placement of other items around the can. The other object near the tin can will show their reflection on it. Place a brightly colored object nearby like a box, and play with the reflections.

Your still life set up should be about 2 to 4 feet away from you. You should have good lighting for the objects that you are painting. This painting takes more than just one session. Make sure that you can leave your setup in one place without having to move the items.

Steps to Draw the Tin Can

Start by drawing the tin can and any other objects in your setup on the canvas. Sketch the can, its cast shadow, and the box with light sketchy lines so that you could easily correct them.

Draw the tin can by making ellipses for the top and bottom and then connect them for the sides. This step uses the transparent construction method. The tin can be just a cylinder with ribs. You can make the ellipses by keeping your hand steady as you make a circular motion using your upper arm. Make several ellipses at the top and bottom part of the can.

Then draw the ones in between. Make sure to create an even space for the ribs. Keep your hand steady and try to mimic the ellipses that you drew for the top and bottom of the can. Draw the entire ellipse even though you see only the forward edge in the finished painting. When you fill in the other ellipses, they will look stacked. This creates the ribs of the can.

First Session

1. Find the patches of color.

    When you look at the can, you see gray, but you also see the reflection of other colors. Look at the shapes and patterns of the different values and colors in the can. Try to see it as a paint-by-number painting where you have larger shapes of color that break down into smaller shapes. In the tin, can, you also see bands of colors that move around its contour.

2. Apply the local colors that you see in a thin wash.

    The pattern of the ribs of the can should have light and dark colors which creates a series of dashes. Across the ribs of the can, they stack up like bricks. Do not blend colors, just paint by block using the patterns that you see on the can. Painting metal is about painting patterns. Painting without blending is what makes metal look like a metal.

3. As you paint, look at the can and examine the reflections that you see on its surface.

    Identify the items on the reflection to help you to help you identify the colors that you see on the can. Add the reflection in the dashes along the ribs and be sure to match the color to its nearby source.

4. Make alterations and continue to develop the patterns by using the colors that you see and add them in spots and patches. After you have all the colors blocked in, you can set the canvas aside to dry a little before you continue.

20

Second Session

After a day or two, you can continue with the next session. Some parts of the painting may feel completely dry while others may have started to develop a sticky surface. They will be wet again as soon as you add more paint. This allows you to blend and mix your colors right on the canvas.

Whenever you spend more than one session on a painting, you must use a drying oil medium rather than solvent. A painting medium allows the painting to dry properly. It adds back in a little of the linseed oil that the solvent dissolves out. It allows you to paint with smooth strokes and to blend and it slows the drying time of your painting. If an oil painting dries too quickly, it damages the layers of paint, causing the surface of the painting to crack.

You can make your own medium or you can use a commercially prepared painting medium. Use the painting medium to wet your brush as you work. The medium makes your paint fluid and creamy. It is very different from working with plain solvent, which can make your paint drippy and watery. The oil in the medium also helps to remoisten the previous layers, which allows the new layers to bond with the previous layers.

Continue to apply paint to the canvas, gradually building up the layers. Try to work with patches of color to develop, and refine patterns of value and colors as you work.

If you have an area that you should blend, experiment with blending in a finite area to get the hang of using the medium. Refrain from using blending if you can to help you maintain clear edges and convincing reflections.

Continue to apply a new layer of paint to all parts of the canvas, developing the image as you go.

Finish off the painting by adding the glints of light on the surface of the can. These glints are white and may stand up pinpoint-like from the metal. In creating these glints, just take up a little dab of something white – (even something slightly off-white would do) using a small dry, brush with no solvent on it at all. Just touch the brush to the point you need and leave it alone.

Paint Glass

A glass is a challenging object to paint for beginners because it is transparent yet it reflects image at the same time. It catches the light and reflects it back to you. It can also include dark spots. You can also pick up reflections on the surface of the glass from objects in the room.

To practice painting a glass, start with a simple object like a regular wine glass with no ornaments. Does the same thing as you would do before you start painting. Lay your object on a background and frame your still life using a viewfinder. Once you have framed your still life, sketch the bottle using a wash.

First Session

1. Find the three largest shapes in the glass, and draw them in.
    Sketch in only the largest shapes now. As you establish the major shapes in your glass, try to identify the sources of the reflections that you see. For instance, if you see the reflection of a box in your glass, notice how the glass distorts its shape.
    Try to maintain the same viewpoint to capture the shapes more easily. In painting glass objects, every time you move, the shapes of the reflections in your object change as well.

2. Mix washes for the color of the wine glass and the other parts of your setup area.
    Concentrate first on the largest shapes. Notice that some areas inside the wine glass are a mix of both the color of the wine glass and the color from behind it. Make up these colors and apply them as you see them.

3. After you block in the major shapes in the glass, find the medium shapes and then the smallest   shapes and block them in.

4. Continue to develop the other parts of the canvas so that you have a consistent surface over the whole painting.

Second Session

After a day or two, polish the application of color to the glass using a painting medium. You can apply a relatively thick application of paint to make your wine glass look more fluid and more glass-like. Find the highlights and apply them with tiny points of white paint. If a light reflection on the glass is relatively big, apply a big patch of white on it instead of tiny dots.

Chapter 6. Painting a Portrait

Painting a portrait is one of the most difficult things that you can do. You must be keen in observing the many details that a human face has. If you are unable to capture certain details of a human face, the result will not turn out like your subject.

Although painting portraits can be a bit frustrating in the beginning, with practice you can develop the skills necessary to create a true likeness.

Practice Sketching the Proportions of a Face

You might already be familiar on how you set the outline to check the proportion of a face. It starts with by drawing an oval shape. Then you divide it up for placement of the eyes, nose, mouth, and so on. If you have never tried making a portrait before, you can practice drawing the features of the face first. You can start by drawing the different features of the face. You can draw from photos or from your image in the mirror. Practice drawing eyes, noses, and mouths until you feel comfortable with them.

You can start practicing the proportions of the face by following the steps:

1. Get a real-life picture of a person. You can use your own picture if you want. Just make sure that picture is life size or big enough for you to see the details.

2. Draw an oval on the canvas and look at the picture.

3. To measure the head, take one of your long paintbrushes and put the handle right down the middle of the face, touching the nose. The top end of the brush must stop exactly at the point at the top of the head. Get the measurement from the top of the head until the bottom part of the chin. You can use a ruler, if you find it more comfortable.

4. To find the eye level, measure from top of the head to the middle place between the eyes. Mark your eye level on your oval.

5. Place the handle so that it measures from your eye level to the chin and find the point for the base of the nose; mark this point on the oval.

6. Do the same for the position of the mouth, using the opening of your mouth as the measuring point.

Find the best point of view for a portrait

Portraits come in different positions and different styles. You will see some portraits wherein the head of the person is slightly tilted to one side, and some with just the face; others include the full body, and the list goes on.

Here are three of the most commonly used types of portraits that you can choose from:

- **Profile Portrait**
  A profile is the easiest point of view to portray, because most of the resemblance depends in the contour of the face. Profile paintings are more like mug shots but profile portraits generally do not include the front face. The main concern of the profile is face of the person

- **Full-face Portrait**
  The face of the person portrayed is directly facing the viewer. This type of portrait is the most difficult because the nose is directly pointing at the viewer, which makes it very hard to capture.

- **Three-quarter View Portrait**
  Three-quarter view is falls between the profile and the full-face portrait. This makes the subject look more natural.

For a beginner, the best option among the three would be the three-quarter view. To practice in painting a portrait, it will be best to start drawing a portrait of yourself. All you need is a mirror and you can position yourself in any way you want.

So, to start this activity, place the brush before your nose and turn your head a quarter. For this exercise, turn to your left. Notice how the eye, nose, and mouth level are the same, but your centerline is off to one side. Your centerline is curve and it follows the contours of the face. This curving line starts in the middle of your forehead and ends in the middle of your chin. It gently bends to the left to follow the line of the nose. The right cheek is a wide surface, but the left cheek is reduced.

Find the relative position of your facial features using your paintbrush handle. Hold it horizontally or vertically and see what parts of your features line up with others.

A Self-Portrait in Black and White

It is a good start to learn and study portraits by drawing a self-portrait because you get to paint whenever you want and virtually wherever you are.

Now the reason that you should start with black and white self-portrait is to simplify things. Master first the art of drawing the different features of your face and then just worry about adding the right colors later.

Work through the following steps to get started:

1. Gather your supplies.
   You need a canvas that is big enough to paint life-size face, a mirror, black and white paint, different types of paintbrush, solvent in a couple of jars, a palette, and a palette knife.

2. Set up your mirror and materials.
   Make sure that you have a three-quarter view of yourself in the mirror. Position a clear light source directed at your face from the side. You need a light source to see the contours of your face. A lamp or a bright window works well.

3. Create your wash.
   Mix up some light gray paint to make a wash and draw an oval on your canvas. Draw the proportions of your face. Your oval must be of the same size as your face to make it easier for you to paint.

4. Make a light line for the level of the eyes, nose, and mouth, and draw the location of the hairline. Check your work and make any necessary corrections.

26

Draw the big contour of the face

After drawing in the proportions of your face, draw a line for the outline that you see on the far side of the face. This contour line is important for finding the placement of the facial features. Follow these steps to find the outline of your face:

1. Begin from the top of the forehead, and curve the line outward to the brow.

2. Dip the line in to follow the hollow of your eye socket.

3. Make a curve line out for the cheekbone and down along the line of the cheek then gently curve in to the chin.

4. Connect the line of the chin in to join the neck. Do not worry if the chin extends beyond the initial oval that you drew.

Fill in the back of the head

The next step is to add some volume to the back of the head.

1. Draw a circular shape from the top of the head near the hairline. Make sure that the line will connect the head with the bottom of the ear. Just make an approximate line of your hair hides this part of your head.
2. Line up this point to the level of the lip line to be more precise.
3. Draw in the outline of the neck under the chin and draw another line from the back of the head.

Work on the contour of the nose

Create the outline of your nose by making another line with your wash. You draw this from your left eyebrow to the base of your nose.

Follow the steps to draw the contour of your nose:

1. Start at the point that is close to the contour of the side of your face. This is the part where the eyebrow extends the farthest.

2. Follow the contour of your eyebrow to the bridge of your nose. Then continue down to the angle of the nose until you reach base of your nose.

3. Add your philtrum. The philtrum is the vertical indentation between the base of the nose and the border of the upper lip.

Add in the features

Now, you add and enhance the other features of the face like the eyes and the mouth. When you draw an eye, the shape resembles to an almond with a round dark shade in the middle and a black dot for the pupil. However, the shape of the eyes look different in a three-quarter portrait which means that you also need to have a different approach to capture them.

Below are the steps to draw an eye for a three-quarter view:

1. Locate the iris of the eye on the far side of your face and put it in using the contour of the nose to help you place it. Your iris should appear as if it is tucked into the bridge of your nose.

2. Then draw your eyelids exactly as how they appear.

3. Draw a line to help you locate the corner of the lips. The far side of your lips should be smaller and the nearside will appear to be a bit bigger.

4. Find the points for the corners of the mouth, and then locate the centreline. Connect the two corners of your mouth using a line. The centerline of your mouth is a continuation of the philtrum.

5. Use the near corner of your lips as a guide to line up the position of the near eye. The corner of the near eye is above the corner of the mouth.

6. To help you find the width of your near eye, measure the base of the nose and the width of the mouth.

7. Check the position of your own face and make necessary adjustments on your painting to refine your features.

Develop the lights and darks of your face

1. Mix three pools of gray paint in different values. You must have a mixture of light gray, medium gray and dark gray. Use a different brush for each mix to avoid color contamination.
2. Find the shaded or dark part of your face and paint the dark gray in those areas.
3. Find the lightest areas of your face gray and paint them with the light gray. Do not blend, just work up the face in patches of light and dark gray.
4. Fill in the middle tones using the medium gray.
5. Cover the rest of the face with the appropriate grays.

Colored Self-Portrait

There are different types of skin tone and every individual has a different skin tone.

Flesh Tones

The human skin has the colors of the primary colors. As you work with oil paints, you will find out that a natural brown is a product of blues, yellows, and reds mixed in the right proportions. You can come up with various skin colors by varying the ratio of the three primary colors, and adding white.

Below are the colors mainly used for flesh skin tones:

- **Yellow**
  Yellow is widely used painting portraits. If you want dark skin, you may use raw or burnt umber.
- **Red**
  Crimson works best for a dark skin tone while red is best for a florid complexion.
- **Blue**
  Deep blue dulls the brilliance of the orange and when you mix the blue and orange, the hue would look for natural.
- **Titanium white**
  When it comes to skin tones titanium white is the best white to use.

Skin Formula

The skin has two basic tones: the light tone and the dark tone. Once you know the basic color combinations that make up these tones, it will be easy for you to come up with a more natural-looking skin.

- **Lighter Skin Tone Formula**
  Start by creating bright orange or you use a ready to use orange oil paint. To create a bright orange, mix yellow and red. Compare the shade of orange with the skin tone you are painting to see if you need to add more yellow or more red. You can adjust the hue by adding white to achieve a tone similar you what you see on a real person, with the lower portion of the check or and the inside of the arm lighter. You will notice that the mixture will be very light and odd to be a skin color. Now to make it look more like a natural skin color, you can add blue.

- **Darker Skin Tone Formula**
  Start with an orange oil paint. You can use an oil paint straight from a tube but the thing about it is, you will still be needing to make adjustments to it anyway so might as well just mix your own orange color. Compare your orange to the skin tone that you are painting. Check if they both lean toward yellow or red.

  Add blue to darken a skin tone or tones you can also try raw and burnt umber. Again, for lighter more natural-looking color, you can add white.

You will notice the colors used for both light and dark tones are the same. The only difference between the two is the ratio of the colors used.

One of the common mistakes of beginners is that they rely too much on white to achieve a light skin tone. When one uses too much white it makes the skin tone too pale and looks unnatural. Adding orange to it makes it more natural looking.

Normally the color of the skin of a person changes when exposed to a bright light. The color of the skin is warmer when it is lighter and cooler when it is darker. Therefore, when you paint a portrait of a person, you might just be using one tone but it will have different values as well.

Oil Painting: 1-2-3 Easy Techniques To Mastering Oil Painting

Since you have already practiced how to make a self-portrait in black and white and you already know the basic formula for skin tones, you can now start making a colored self-portrait. Incorporate everything that you have learned from blocking in the shaded part of the painting to mixing colors and making a self-portrait.

You should also be more confident now to try other objects for your next oil painting project. Incorporate everything that you have learned in this book. Apply the basic knowledge in blocking in the shaded part of an object, different glazing techniques to make corrections, and using complimentary colors to add more complexity to your painting.

Conclusion

Thank you again for downloading this book!

I hope this book could help you gain confidence in trying oil painting. With everything that this book has imparted you, oil painting should no longer scare or intimidate you.

The basic techniques, discussed in this book should help you resolve your reservations in oil painting. It might be a complicated process but with sufficient knowledge and continuous practice, becoming comfortable with it is not impossible.

The next step you need to do is to buy your supplies and start painting.

Finally, if you enjoyed this book, please take the time to share your thoughts and post a review on Amazon. It'd be greatly appreciated!

Thank you and good luck!

Book 2
Pastel Drawing

By Scott Landowski

1-2-3 Easy Techniques To Pastel Drawing

Table of Contents

Introduction

I want to thank you and congratulate you for downloading the book, "Pastel Drawing: 1-2-3 Easy Techniques to Mastering Pastel Drawing!"

This book contains proven steps and strategies on how to master the pastel medium to create stunning works of art. Art, in all its forms, plays an essential role in making our everyday lives more delightful, satisfactory and inspirational. It affects our mood in a positive way and brings a sense of tranquility that helps us get through some difficult and stressful times. Although art may not be a vital necessity, no one can deny the joy it brings.

Art is also a great way to express ourselves and to translate the beauty in nature that surrounds us. And one of the best forms we can translate it into is a beautiful piece of drawing or painting. Inspiration is everywhere, all that is left for artists to do is to grab a medium and start recording it. To achieve optimal results, what better medium can we use than pastels!

Pastels offer extremely vivid and intense colors that can make your drawings look realistic when done skillfully. The sense of fulfillment you will feel while viewing your finished artwork is undeniable. With the right amount of passion, patience and determination, anyone can master the art of pastel drawing and be an inspiration to others.

To help you achieve just that, this book will provide you with some easy tips, techniques and tutorials that you will surely find beneficial for your development. So, grab your pastels and paper and bring out your artistic side. Now is the best time to show off your pastel drawing skills!

Thanks again for downloading this book, I hope you enjoy it!

Chapter 1: What is a Pastel?

A pastel is an art medium made by mixing pure powdered pigment together with a binder to create a thick paste. The thick paste is then formed into sticks and allowed to dry. Because they are fashioned with almost pure and dry pigment, the color produced by pastels is richer and more intense than that of other art media.

Pastel is also the term used to describe an artwork—can be a drawing or a painting—created using pastel sticks. A "pastelist" is an artist who uses pastels as their medium in creating their artwork.

1.1. Types of Pastels

There are four general types of pastels: hard, soft, pencil, and oil. While they are all basically pigment in the form a stick, they differ in the way by which they are bound together. Hard pastels, soft pastels, and pastel pencils are held together with a water-based binder, usually a gum or resin. On the other hand, oil pastels are bound with an oil-based binder, usually oil or wax. This gives oil pastels a distinct texture comparable to oil paints.

Since hard, soft and pastel pencils are similarly bound, they are compatible with each other and can be worked on the same drawing or painting. Oil pastels, however, can only be worked with alone and cannot be combined with any other pastel types.

You can tell the distinction between these four pastel types by their look and texture.

Here are the main characteristics of each type:

Hard Pastels

Hard pastels contain less pigment and more binder than soft pastels. The more binder they have, the harder they become. This makes the color effect of hard pastels less intense. However, they do not crumble or crack as easily as soft pastels.

Hard pastels are usually cylindrical in shape and are hard and shiny. They can be sharpened using a knife to produce fine lines. Because they are firmer and more stable, hard pastels are particularly suitable for working on location and drawing techniques. Alternatively, the edges of hard pastel sticks can be used to apply extensive swathes of color.

Hard pastels are available in students' and artists' quality, and come in fewer colors than soft pastels. They can be used in blending, and are well-suited for working on small details, initial sketches and finishing touches.

Soft Pastels

Soft pastels, also called chalk pastels or "dry" pastels, are the most commonly used type of pastels. They have highly concentrated pigment that is bound together with the slightest amount of binder possible. The colors of soft pastels are delicately bright and intense. However, since they are dry and do not stick to the surface, they crumble easily and can be brushed off.

Soft pastels look and feel like typical blackboard chalk— soft and powdery with a cylindrical shape. This fragile consistency allows the artist to blend and layer various colors easily on the working surface. This also gives the artist prompt feedback on the colors as they apply them.

Soft pastels are best for beginners. If used with pastel pencils, soft pastels can help you create fine lines. As they are "chalky," you can make minor corrections or erasures which can be difficult to do with oil pastels.

With some manufacturers offering up to 500 colors, soft pastels have the widest selection of colors compared to other pastel types. They also come in a range of sizes: thick sticks, half sticks, and whole sticks.

Deciding between hard and soft pastels depends on the drawing techniques you'd like to make use of. If you're a beginner, you can begin mainly with soft pastels. Invest in a few individual hard pastels so you can try them out and use them for preliminary sketches and fine details.

Pastel Pencils

Pastel pencils are best if you want to create detailed and controlled artworks with pastels. They are versatile and can be used in combination with soft or hard pastels. You can use them wet or dry and they work well in blending technique. Pastel pencils can be sharpened to a point to draw precise and defined details. They are also recommended for basic sketching and drawing.

Pastel pencils look much like traditional pencils, but enclosed within the wood is a thin pastel stick with a consistency between soft and hard pastels. They are convenient to use as they are neat, unlike soft pastels. With pastel pencils, you can create quick sketches or drawings without much preparation or clean-up. This makes them suitable for working outdoors.

Oil Pastels

Oil pastels are like oil paints in terms of versatility and texture. But unlike oil paints, oil pastels don't have smelly chemicals and don't harden or dry out completely. As compared to soft pastels which produce more delicate and softer hue, oil pastels create brighter, more intense hue that makes them suitable for rough, bold and expressive work.

Oil pastels can also be worked, thinned, and diluted like oil paintings. They are round-shaped and have a wax-like, creamy consistency, making them easily distinguishable from soft pastels. They are also more stable and adhere to the working surface better than soft pastels.

Oil pastels do not require fixatives. They do not smudge, crumble, or release fine dust into the air which can result to respiratory irritation, whereas soft pastels often do. For this reason, and due to their non-toxic properties, oil pastels are the preferred type of pastel to be used in schools.

Oil pastels can also be great for beginners as it doesn't necessarily require setting up various solutions, brushes or other tools. All you need to get started are your oil pastel sticks and a sheet of paper to work on, and you're good to go.

Like other pastel types, oil pastels also come in either students' quality or artists' quality. Cheaper oil pastels have a look and feel like kids' crayons. They don't produce the same effect as artist quality pastels. This is frustrating to artists who are new to oil pastels and they often switch to other medium without discovering the real essence of oil pastels. So, if you're interested in trying out oil pastels, you need to be mindful of the difference between these two qualities. The difference alone could be the key factor in deciding whether you should continue using oil pastels.

1.2. Drawing Materials

To get started with pastel drawing, all you basically need is a set of pastels and a pastel paper to work on. However, due to the wide selections of drawing materials available on the market, a beginner can get confused and overwhelmed. To help you out, here is a list of art materials you need and some buying tips:

A Set of Pastels

Although there are many different choices available, choosing a set of pastel is quite easy. When you use pastels in drawing, you don't really want to blend individual colors too much as they tend to lose their brilliance or vibrancy if you do. So, in choosing a set of pastels, you would want to get the largest set you can afford to buy, with the most number of colors. This is to reduce the frequency of blending you would have to do.

Another factor to consider is how the colors are grouped in the various sets. Choosing a set really depends on your subject taste. Some sets are grouped with colors that would be used for purposes such as for drawing landscapes, portraits, seascapes, and the like. Some sets consist of general colors.

Pastel Paper

The paper you need to use for pastel drawing needs to have the required roughness (called the paper's "tooth") on which the pastel will adhere. The surface of an ordinary writing paper is too smooth and it doesn't allow the pastel to grip onto it. So, in buying paper for pastel drawing, always choose paper that is manufactured specifically for pastel work.

Pastel papers are fashioned in various ways to give different levels of texture and tooth. You can experiment with several pastel papers with varying textures and tooth until you find the one that suits your taste best.

Other Drawing Materials

While pastel sticks and paper are the basic materials you need in drawing, there are also other art materials you can make use of to aid in achieving better results.

- Charcoal sticks for preliminary sketches and drawings

- A clean cloth or wet wipes for cleaning up

- Sand paper for layered/textured drawings

- Gloves for skin protection

- Brushes for special effects and blending

- Bread for erasures

- Pastel stick holder

- Cotton buds to blend small areas

- A blending stump or a tissue to blend tones and colors

- Craft knife to trim paper to desired size and for special effects

- For other special effects, you may use a soft eraser, a sponge and toilet paper

- A can of fixative spray to protect your artwork and prevent it from being ruined by careless smudging (a hair spray can also be used as an alternative)

1.3.   Pastel Quality

Pastels, like other art media, come in different levels of quality. Generally, there are two main pastel grades: students' quality and artists' quality. Students' quality pastels are less expensive and usually have low quality pigments. They are also made with more binder and filler which make the colors less intense and vibrant. However, they do not easily crumble like artist grade pastels. Artists' quality pastels, on the other hand, contain stronger and more tightly-bound pigments. The pigment and binder are more proportional which makes the color bolder and more intense. Artists' quality pastels also have a wider selection of colors and are more fade-resistant than student grade pastels.

Beginners and intermediate artists who are not yet willing to invest in more expensive quality pastels can begin with the students' set. But if you are serious about pastel drawing, buy the artists' quality pastels and you will see a great difference with the results.

1.4.   Pastel Colors

You can blend pastel colors but you cannot mix them as well as you can with paint. To make up for this, a wide range of colors is made available on the market. You can purchase pastels individually or in sets. If you're a beginner and unsure as to which pastel type you want to invest in, you can begin by getting yourself individual pastels which will also keep your expenses low. Once you have figured which type you really want to buy, you can get a set of pastels that contains a good range of colors. You can also choose and customize your own set of colors.

Some artist grade pastels contain rare pigments which make them costlier than others. Alternatively, some student grade pastels contain artificial pigments which imitate the color of the more expensive natural pigments. If you see the word "hue" after the pigment name, it means that the pigment of the pastel is made using a cheaper substitute.

1.5.   Health and Safety

Pastels, especially soft pastels, are a dry medium and often deposit airborne dust which you can inhale as you work. This dust can cause respiratory discomfort and can be quite dangerous. To avoid inhaling pastel dust, work in a well-ventilated room. You can also wear face masks or get an air purifier to make you less exposed to dust.

Some pastels also contain toxic pigments like cadmium. Exposure to cadmium can lead to cadmium poisoning. To avoid this, buy only non-toxic pastels which are   available   at   any   local   art   supply   store.

Chapter 2: Techniques for Pastel Drawing

The techniques for pastel drawing can be quite difficult to master especially for beginners. Unlike in painting, you cannot test the colors on a palette first before applying them to the surface, but rather you mix and blend the medium directly on the drawing surface. Also, en error in pastel drawing cannot be concealed the way an error in painting can be painted out.

Anyhow, there are various ways by which you can apply pastels to a surface. Some of these techniques can help you get away with errors. There is no right or wrong way in carrying out these techniques. You should simply select the technique that is most appropriate for your desired effect. For most pastel drawings, you can use these techniques in combination with each other.

2.1. Blending

Blending is probably the most common and basic technique for pastel drawing. Blending happens when different pastel colors are applied in layers on the same area. You can smooth the transition between tones and colors by rubbing or smearing the pastel into the drawing surface. You can accomplish this using your finger, a tissue, blending stump, soft brush or cotton swab. You can use your finger for blending on large areas. But for smaller areas, use a blending stump or ear buds instead.

When you blend, and rub over the colors, you will notice that their vibrancy tends to diminish. Here is a way to overcome this: once you have blended the colors with your finger or a stump, gently rub the original colors on top of them to create a thin vibrant layer. This will help maintain the vibrancy of the pastel and achieve better results.

2.2. Scumbling

Scumbling is a pastel technique in which thin but opaque layers of pastel are applied over the top of previously worked areas. This creates a partial covering and allows bits of the pastel underneath the new color to shine through. This technique produces visually stimulating results and is often used when working with landscapes and other natural scenes and objects.

When scumbling is done, the overlapping colors visually "mix" and cause the viewer to perceive a new color. This is often referred to as *optical color mixing*. For instance, if blue streaks are applied next to, or over yellow streaks, it creates a perception of green.

As you have imagined, the tooth or texture of the paper is one of the factors that affect the process of scumbling. So, to achieve the desired effect of scumbling, consider the tooth or texture of the paper that you will use.

2.3.   Stippling

Stippling is a common drawing technique used to create areas of light and shade by dotting the medium down onto the working surface. This process is repeated until the desired effect is created. The more compressed the dots are, the darker the area will be. This technique works well in painting as well as in pastel drawing. It can also be done with other drawing media such as charcoal, crayons, and conte crayons.

Stippling can create an optical illusion when done by a skilled artist. From a distant view, the areas in which the shading was created will look like a smooth application of pastels. The dots will only be apparent when surveyed very closely.

2.4.   Hatching

Hatching has 6 basic forms: *parallel hatching, contour hatching, cross hatching, fine cross hatching, tick hatching*, and *woven hatching*. Hatching techniques are used to create value, texture and the optical illusion of light and form by drawing lines close together in similar or various directions. Aside from pastels, these linear techniques also work well with many other drawing media such as colored pencils, graphite, and pen and ink. Hatching can also be observed in traditional techniques for printmaking such as engraving and etching.

Parallel Hatching

Parallel hatching is a basic form of hatching that uses non-crossing lines to demonstrate the value (light and shadow) on or round an object in a drawing. Hatching consists of sets of parallel lines positioned closely together. The areas where you place hatching will appear shaded and darker, and the areas where you don't will give the impression of a featured highlight.

Contour Hatching

Instead of using simple parallel lines, it is sometimes necessary to curve the lines and adhere to the contours of an object. This is referred to as *contour hatching*. In addition to creating value, contour hatching technique also enhances the volume and dimensionality of the object you are drawing.

Cross Hatching

After drawing one set of lines, you may add another set of lines on top to add more value to your hatching. The second set of lines can be drawn diagonally or perpendicularly to the first set, and can be another set of parallel lines of curved lines to adhere to the contours of the object. This cross-hatching technique is an effective way to create density variations and to deepen the values in your drawing.

Fine Cross Hatching

Fine cross hatching is the richest and most delicate hatching technique. It is done using the same method as above, consisting of various layers of cross hatching instead of only two, to create more gradations in value and tone. In fine cross hatching, a fine-line pencil or the edge of a hard-pastel stick is best used to draw more detailed and precise lines that will seem to blend together when viewed from far away.

Tick Hatching

Tick hatching is composed of short parallel marks or "ticks" that are piled over one another to produce variations in density. This technique works best with a broader pen or pastel to enhance the graphic quality of your drawing.

Woven Hatching

Woven hatching is also referred to as *basket hatching*. This technique provides very striking effects and enhances the graphic quality of your work when done correctly. To do this technique, draw a short set of parallel lines in the same direction, then another set of parallel lines in an almost-perpendicular or diagonal direction. The effect of this technique will look woven (thus the name) when used correctly. The marks can also be cross-hatched to create more density and achieve your desired effect.

2.5. Scratching

The technique of scratching gives your drawings added details that are simple but unique. To do this, lay down two or more contrasting colors before doing the main drawing. The greater the number of colors you lay, the greater the range of colors that will be revealed upon scratching. The result is more effective if the color of the final layer on top is dark. To do the scratching part, you need to make use of a scratching tool. It can be a needle, a painting knife, or a comb. If you don't have any of these tools, you can also sharpen your pastel stick to a point and use it to scratch out the image.

2.6. Feathering

Feathering is a drawing technique that usually uses layers of short strokes that may overlap or cross on top of each other. The lines that are drawn may also curve to adhere to the contours of an object in your drawing, and this adds to the illusion of light and form. Like scumbling, feathering can also provide vibrancy to your work, and result to optical color mixing in which the colors are visually mixed instead of being physically blended on the drawing surface.

This technique is particularly good for providing the glistening appearance of feathers, scales, and fabric, or for creating effects that are distinctive with light.

2.7.   Other Tips and Techniques

There are three ways to use a pastel: by drawing with the end, the edge, or the side. Hold the pastel stick as you would hold a pen or pencil and it will create a great expression that suggests a sense of the gesticulation you made. You can vary the breadth of the line by applying alternate pressure to the pastel. The more pressure you apply, the more pastel you will be laying down on the surface. To create thinner lines, apply the pastel more lightly on the paper or you can also use the edge of the stick.

For detail work, you can create finer lines using the sharp edge of a new pastel stick. When it becomes blunt through use, you can re-sharpen it with a cutter or knife. You can also reshape the pastel stick by scraping it against a rough surface such as sandpaper. While most artists use pastel pencils to create more precise lines, learning this technique helps especially when you don't have a pencil available and need to draw finer marks.

If you want to create broad streaks of color quickly, you can draw with the side of the stick. For better results, split the stick in two and use one half of it. Alter the pressure to produce varying gradations of texture on the paper. When the side of the stick has eroded due to constant use, it will leave two sharp edges which you can then use to draw finer lines.

As previously mentioned, you can use a combination of any of these techniques in the same drawing. It is necessary to incorporate various strokes and marks in any image. Regardless of which technique/s you use, the goal is to always create established layers of various colors on the pastel paper. This provides depth in your work and enhances the illusion of light and form. Practice these easy techniques to further develop your artistic skills and to create successful pieces of pastel artwork.

Chapter 3: Basic Tips and Tutorials

Pastels can be a challenging medium to master. Their loose characteristic makes it difficult to control on the drawing surface. For this reason, beginners are often discouraged that they tend to dismiss this medium after only a few tries and move on to something else. This is unfortunate as many new artists miss out on the opportunity of discovering how great pastels can be. They shun the medium that might have been perfect for them if only they worked with it a little longer.

So, if you're new to pastels, keep working and don't limit yourself. Pastel drawing can be fulfilling. You can even discover new techniques of your own as you move along. Having said that, here are some basic tutorials, as well as some tips, to get you started with the amazing world of pastel drawing.

3.1. Landscapes

One of the most common subjects of artists for their drawings are landscapes, and it is no wonder. As artists, we are moved by the natural beauty that surrounds us and interpreting them into beautiful works of art is the least we can do. Landscapes are overflowing with interesting shapes, lines, and varied colors. These elements often arrange themselves into visually appealing compositions and the artist will simply need to record them in the form of a drawing or a painting.

Pastels are inherently loose which makes them the perfect medium for interpreting natural sceneries such as landscapes. In this tutorial, we will record a typical, natural landscape with the use of soft pastels. Work on an orange pastel paper that has a rough texture (tooth) as this tutorial calls for heavy layering. The heavy tooth of the surface allows you to apply multiple layers of color without upsetting the tooth. This is essential for the coherent reception of the material.

Moving on, here are the steps in creating a beautiful landscape artwork:

- To begin, work a layer of darker blue over a layer of lighter blue pastels. This will form the background of the landscape. The light blue pastel creates the outlines for the clouds and develops the transition from light to dark. Use your finger to gently blend the colors of the clouds.

- Create a line for the distant row of trees. This should overlap the background. Apply a dark yellow-green pastel to begin. Then apply burnt umber followed by a light mark of black. Blend the colors gently with your finger and leave a hard edge on top of the row of trees.

- Next, to form the distant ground, use a variety of yellow-greens, followed by yellow-ochre, light cream, and a few bands of Burnt Sienna. This creates shapes of color that are aligned horizontally.

- Add several distant trees. Do not worry about the details. Instead, focus on the values, shapes and colors that are created.

- Apply a fair amount of light cream into the middle ground and allow tiny portions of the orange pastel paper to show through. Apply a few bands of burnt sienna for added color.

- Still working on the middle ground, apply patches of red over layers of purple, then darken it with burnt umber. This will form the grasses for the landscape. Use dark yellow-green pastel to draw smaller grasses and highlight it with a lighter yellow-green.

- Continue adding some more details to the image such as formations of rocks with small trees and bits of grass behind them. As you reach the closer ground or the foreground, make the lines for the grass longer and more precise. Use different colors and create variations in value to make your drawing appear more animated.

- Draw additional strokes with light cream pastel to imply the field of grass. Leave some recesses to reveal portions of the darker layers' underneath. You can also use a lighter cream pastel to highlight the tips of the taller grass blades.

- Going back to the background, grab a white pastel to intensify the colors of the clouds. Gently blend the new colors with the previously applied colors using your finger.

Your landscape drawing is now complete! You can finish off your work by spraying fixative all over it. You can also use a hairspray as an alternative. Fixative spray protects your work and prevents it from smudging.

3.2. Seascapes

Your repertoire as an artist will not be complete if you are not able to draw seascapes. This subject matter can be tricky as oceans are continually moving and your drawing needs to capture that illusion for it to be successful. Additionally, it can be quite difficult to draw if your target is always moving.

If you're a beginner, you can start with an image reference as an alternative. Learn and understand the basics of creating the illusion of waves and you can draw them easily. For seascapes, the same with landscapes, it is recommended to use a surface that has a heavy tooth as this subject often requires substantial applications of layering. You can use soft, hard or oil pastels, depending on your preference. As you move along, apply these tips to achieve appealing and desirable results:

- Scrutinize the subject very closely and you will be able to identify the directional lines, as well as the colors, values and tones being used. These elements are all essential to create the effect you are after. Place colors and values in the right locations within your drawing to give the viewer the illusion that they are seeing actual waves.

- Consider the sequence in which you are to draw the subject. Typically, pastelist commence the drawing by working on the background. Then develop the middle ground and foreground over the accomplished background. In this manner, you will be able to layer the colors in a more effective way.

- Create a great extent of value (the lightness and shadiness of a color) within your drawing. Value plays a vital role in the way we perceive things. Use different tones and shades from the same color group and it will help you achieve the illusion you're trying to make. For instance: although the ocean is generally blue, use other tones such as blue-green, green, dark blue, light blue and so on. Layer these colors and their values and it will aid in creating the illusion of moving water.

- Another important factor to consider is the directional lines. Since we are working with waves, observe the contrast between horizontal and diagonal lines. These are examples of contour lines for which you can use the layering techniques you have learned so far.

- Apply your medium in a manner that it adheres to the curves and contours which characterize the subject. Work with the contours of the waves to effectively bring about the effect you're after.

Due to its simplicity and seemingly unvarying color, the ocean might look like a simple thing to draw. But the challenge is to capture the illusion of movement and gleam of the waves within your drawing, and drive the viewer into believing that the waves are moving. With a little practice and enhancement of skills, you will eventually be able to pull it off quite easily.

3.3. Clouds

Another basic subject that a pastelist should master is the clouds. Landscapes and other scenes often require the presence of the sky. While a cloudless and still sky is easier to accomplish, —only some basic blending and layering of the medium will be enough—a scene that calls for clouds can become more complicated. Here are few useful tips to help you create more realistic-looking clouds.

- When you are drawing clouds, the first thing you should remember is that clouds are three-dimensional objects. Consequently, they will often have a shaded part and a highlighted part. It is essential to create the illusion of shadows and highlights to produce more natural and realistic clouds.

- Clouds take on various forms and shapes. This gives you the freedom to be loose and diverse when you're making the outlines of the marks. Exercise this freedom as this will promote the illusion and effect of organic shapes.

- As with most subject matters, it is important to observe value. Endeavor to incorporate a greater extent of value in any of your drawings. As clouds are often blue and white, you can use other tones such as gray, dark blue, light blue and the like, to create the illusion of three-dimensionality and dynamism.

These tips are important to remember not only for clouds, but for all types of subject matters. Apply these tips and in no time, you will master the creation of realistic-looking clouds.

Landscapes, seascapes and clouds may seem basic, but pulling them off convincingly requires skills and thorough understanding of the art. Exercise your creativity and adroitness in every artwork you are working on. With a good selection of medium and application of techniques, you can turn from a novice pastelist to a competent and skillful artist.

Chapter 4: Portrait Drawing with Pastels

Portrait drawing is a traditional art form. After all, what better subject can an artist have but themselves and the people around them? Whether you're drawing a self-portrait, a portrait of a loved one, or a stranger's perhaps, there are two main factors you should be mindful about: the proportions of the human face and the accuracy of your drawing to those proportions. In this chapter, we will study the basic rules of symmetry for the human face, which all pastelist, painters and artists alike must learn and understand. The other sections will provide you with simple approaches to drawing realistic eyes, nose, lips and ears.

4.1. Understanding Facial Proportions

Drawing a portrait is rather like drawing any other types of subject matter. You must scrutinize the subject so that you can draw the features accurately. The goal is to always make the closest resemblance possible between the portrait and the subject. To do this, it is important to understand facial proportions first.

Proportion is the relation of one part to another or to the whole with respect to placement and size. Generally, human faces follow the same rules of symmetry but many people still make mistakes when drawing the human face due to their lack of understanding of the facial symmetry. When drawing a face, follow these basic rules to get the job done correctly:

- First thing to keep in mind is that the eyes are always found in the middle of the face. People tend to make mistakes on this and incorrectly position the eyes way up the forehead. You can draw a horizontal line halfway in the middle of the face to serve as the "eye line" and position the eyes there.

- Typically, the width of a human face is five times the width of a single eye. Of course, you need to draw only two eyes. The concept of "five eyes" should serve as a guide to help you determine the correct width of the face.

- When drawing a line for the nose, it should run from the center of the eye line down to the bottom of the face. When drawing the actual nose, it should be thinnest between the eyes and growing a bit wider down the nostrils. There are exceptions to this, of course. Obviously, everyone has a unique nose. Some noses are longer, some are wider, some are thinner, and so on. So, you really need to pay attention to the details of your subject's nose to capture it more accurately.

- Each inside corner of the eyes typically aligns with either edge of the nose, while each pupil of the eyes typically aligns with either corner of the mouth.

50

- The line for the mouth runs from the center of the nose line down the bottom of the face. This line indicates the location where the top and bottom lip meet.

- Typical ears are positioned between the nose line and the eye line.

Keep these simple basics in mind and use them as a guide to help you draw a properly proportioned face. Most importantly, study the face of your subject carefully to get more precise results. These are only standard rules that may be applicable to most people, but not to everyone.

4.2. Drawing the Eye

As the saying goes, eyes are the windows to the soul. Amongst all facial features, the eyes are the most expressive. When you're drawing the subject's eyes, it will be more convincing if you can resemble not only the physical characteristics of the eyes but also the emotions that may hide behind them. To draw an eye that looks realistic, here is a step-by-step approach:

- To begin, sketch the outlines of the shape of the eye using a skin-tone color first, then a dark brown.

- Layer the colors in the iris of the eye. Apply green, blue, and a bit of yellow then blend the colors with your finger.

- Next, layer the darker values and tones of the iris over the initial colors. You can use blue and dark brown for this. Layering is always essential in any drawing. It creates depth and makes the colors look more convincing and realistic.

- Apply additional colors directly upon the darker layer, but this time, less mixing and smudging is needed. You can use light blue and yellow-green for this.

- Highlight some of the areas in the iris part of the eye with a light cream. You can also use this color in the white areas of the eyes.

- Apply some marks with red, cream, and red-orange. This is to indicate the edges of the eye.

- Layer white on top of the slightly darker values of the white areas of the eye. This creates a highlight and makes the eye look moist. You can also use white on top of the iris to make it look "sparkly."

- Apply skin-tone colors round the eye. Work the colors into the surface as you apply them.

- Continue to add and blend the skin-tone colors into the working surface.

51

- Finally, add the eyelashes with a black pencil. A nicely sharpened pastel pencil will create more precise-looking eyelashes.

Your realistic eye drawing is now complete! As always, a careful study of your subject's facial features should be done to make the finished work more accurate.

4.3. Drawing the Nose

Drawing noses is easier than you may think. Many people seem to struggle with this part but it's rather simple. Here are the basics:

- To begin, draw four curved lines: two lines for the nostrils, two lines for the edges of the nose.

- Apply darker values on the shaded areas of the nose. Begin with the darkest areas then to the midtones. You can do this with a pencil first.

- Continue to add shading on the right locations of the nose to make the illusion that there is a source of light. Do not add more marks or lines. Focus on shading the dark areas while leaving some of the areas slightly untouched.

- Adding more value will make your nose look more realistic. Light areas of the nose will appear protruded, while the dark areas will look like they're way at the back.

- Look for the light and dark areas on your subject's nose and draw them as you see them. By doing this, your nose will appear lifelike.

Isn't that easy? All you need to draw are four simple lines and the rest is shading and adding value. As for the shape, size and length of the nose, it really depends on your subject. There is no specific formula when it comes to drawing noses, you should observe your subject closely and draw the specifications that you will see.

4.4. Drawing the Lips

Some people seem to have problems when it comes to drawing the lips or mouth. This is mainly because everyone has a unique set of lips. So, there is no definite method for drawing the lips but there are some things you can consider that may make the task easier.

- Observation is the key. Every set of lips is different. Whether your subject is a live person or from a photo reference, it is always important to scrutinize each feature to get the exact size, shape, color and curves of the lips.

- Use contour lines to aid in outlining the shape of the lips. Also, apply the layering techniques you have learned from the previous chapters to make the lips look believable. Apply the pastels onto the working area using contour lines, as well.

- At the beginning, it is okay to be loose with your drawing. Forming the shape of the lips might call for some mistakes and that is fine, so long as you get the correct form. Especially when you're using soft pastels, you can remedy the mistakes later. Keep your working area clean but do not worry too much about stray lines and marks.

- Pastel drawing requires several layering, particularly with soft pastels. You may need to do more layering to get the result that you want so don't get frustrated if your work doesn't look developed enough after only a few layers. Establish the colors and always keep your cool.

4.5. Drawing the Ears

As with all facial features, ears vary in sizes and shapes. Pay close attention to the shapes and lines of your subject's ears and draw them exactly as you see them. Drawing realistic ears is simple. You only need to draw the outlines or contours of your subject's ears and the rest is shading and adding value (same as with drawing noses). As there is no definite formula regarding drawing ears, remember these basic tips instead to accomplish the job more effectively:

- Be familiar with the proper location of the ears. As discussed earlier, ears are typically positioned between the nose line and the eye line. Be careful not to place them way below the nose or way above the eyes as they will not look properly proportioned if you do.

- Keep in mind that every set of ears is unique, as all facial features are. Learn to analyze and examine even the subtlest details that are present on every subject and from every angle. Little details can make a difference with the outcome.

- Remember that ears are complementary features of the portrait—they are not the main subject. Sometimes, the ears are completely or partially covered either by the subject's hair or any other accessory the subject may be wearing. Do not become too preoccupied with working with the ears that you overlook the whole picture.

Drawing the facial features often follow the same basic rules. And in all your drawings, never miss to observe each feature of your subject's face to capture its unique specifics.

Hopefully by now you have already drawn a realistic portrait with all the facial features properly positioned. As you will notice, one great thing about the pastel medium is that it gives the artists the best of both worlds. Although we generally call it "drawing," the results often look like they are "painted" instead of drawn. This is due to the vivid and vibrant colors that pastels often contain. In fact, pastel-drawn artworks are usually called "painting."

Now that you have learned the basics of portrait drawing with pastels, why don't you invite a friend or a loved one to become the subject for your drawings? A truly skillful artist can not only draw a good portrait that resembles the subject, but can also capture the character and personality of the subject in their drawings. Now this may sound too demanding but with a creative mind and passionate will, the possibilities are limitless!

Chapter 5: An Overview of Still Life Drawing

Although it may not always be the most interesting subject, drawing still life can be quite exciting. It is good practice for developing and enhancing observational skills, as well as interpretative skills of an artist. With still life, you can learn how to perceive objects like an artist—with a mindful awareness of their shape, tone, texture, color, form, outline, proportions and composition.

5.1. What is Still Life?

But what really is still life? To say simply, still life is an arrangement or a scene of inanimate objects that are either painted or drawn from observation. Still life arrangement can be composed of related or unrelated objects. The goal is to create an artwork that is skillfully constructed, thought provoking and aesthetically pleasing.

Contrary to landscape painting or drawing, still life subjects give artists more freedom to create the picture and decide on its compositions before painting or drawing anything. Traditionally, objects that comprise still life arrangements include foods, flowers, glasses, bottles and vases. Some modern artists, however, have averted from tradition and they are more liberated in choosing their subjects.

5.2. The Rule of Odds

The Rule of Odds applies to all forms of visual arts—photography, sculpture, graphic design and painting. This rule states that objects grouped together will look more interesting and appealing if they have an odd number. Viewers, for some reason, would rather look at a composition of "3" objects instead of "2," or "5" rather than "4."

The human eye has the tendency to wander to the middle of the group. If it sees an even number of objects, it will end up looking at the blank center and this inhibits eye movement.

When composing a still life arrangement, strive to apply the Rule of Odds to achieve a more aesthetically pleasing composition. If you have one main object, complement it with two or four supporting objects so one of them will be the center.

Still life has given artists a platform to explore their association with the objects that exist in their world. Practice drawing with still life objects to improve your techniques and further develop your skills as an artist.

Conclusion

Thank you again for downloading this book!

I hope this book could unleash the artist in you and inspire you to become a better, more competent pastel list.

The possibilities with respect to creating art are seemingly endless! In our world filled with beauty and wonder, you will never run out of inspiration. The marvelous scenes of nature, the picturesque views of our surroundings, and the smiles of our loved ones are all too inciting not to draw and capture every moment of.

But art isn't only about interpreting the world in which we live in. It is also a great way to express our inner thoughts and feelings about life. Our dreams, memories, longings, fears and joy can also be translated into wondrous artworks. Art is a means of self-expression that lets the audience peek into the world within us. What a nice feeling it is when you can just let everything out!

Everywhere we go, art is evident, inspiring us in many ways, influencing us to become a better person. It is amazing to know that with only a piece of paper in hand and a simple medium such as a pastel, we can pay tribute to all the beautiful things that life has given us, in a creative and passionate way.

Now, the next step is to keep moving forward. Practice your pastel drawing skills and never be afraid to take it to the next level. If at first you don't achieve the result that you want, do not dwell on the frustration and do better next time. A pastel drawing master was once a beginner who failed but didn't give up. Keep pushing yourself to the limit. Do not hold back. Be bolder. Let your creativity overflow. Who knows, you might just one day be lined up with all the world's greatest pastel artists!

Finally, if you enjoyed this book, please take the time to share your thoughts and post a review on Amazon. It'd be greatly appreciated!

Thank you and good luck!

www.ingramcontent.com/pod-product-compliance
Lightning Source LLC
Chambersburg PA
CBHW071819170526
45167CB00003B/1367